CONTENTS

Words that look like **this** are explained in the glossary on page 31.

DISCOVERING
DINOSAURS

For over 140 million years, dinosaurs ruled the Earth's land. Experts think that there may have been around 2,000 different **species**, but, of these, only around 1,000 have been discovered and named. Here are some of the things that dinosaurs had in common.

ALL TRUE DINOSAURS WERE reptiles AND THEY LIVED ON LAND.

All dinosaurs laid eggs, from which their babies hatched.

DINOSAURS WALKED ON TWO OR FOUR LEGS.

DINOSAURS

by
Joanna Brundle

Photo Credits

Images are courtesy of Shutterstock.com. With thanks to Getty Images, Thinkstock Photo and iStockphoto.

Cover – David Herraez Calzada, 2 – Herschel Hoffmeyer, 4&5 – Yellow Cat, Svetlana Monyakova, Herschel Hoffmeyer, Daniel Eskridge, 6&7 – Photomontage, paleontologist natural, Marcio Jose Bastos Silva, Alex Coan, 8&9 – EA230311, Designua, Daniel Eskridge, 10&11 – Daniel Eskridge, Warpaint, kamomeen, AKKHARAT JARUSILAWONG, 12&13 – Daniel Eskridge, Kostyantyn Ivanyshen, Herschel Hoffmeyer, Martina Badini, 14&15 – Daniel Eskridge, Warpaint, 16&17 – Warpaint, Daniel Eskridge, Herschel Hoffmeyer, 18&19 – Michael Rosskothen, Daniel Eskridge, Elenarts, Danny Ye, 20&21 – Daniel Eskridge, Michael Rosskothen, Warpaint, Herschel Hoffmeyer, 22&23 – Daniel Eskridge, AKKHARAT JARUSILAWONG, 24&25 – MikhailSh, Kostyantyn Ivanyshen, AKKHARAT JARUSILAWONG, Michael Rossjothen, 26&27 – gorosan, Daniel Eskridge, Catmando, Giedriius, 28&29 – dubes sonego, Anna Durinikova, Warpaint, Tokareva Irina, 30&31 – Mopic, Herschel Hoffmeyer.

BookLife
PUBLISHING

©2021
BookLife Publishing Ltd.
King's Lynn
Norfolk PE30 4LS

ISBN: 978-1-83927-144-1

Written by:
Joanna Brundle

Edited by:
William Anthony

Designed by:
Gareth Liddington

There were many dinosaur species, and they all looked very different from each other. They ranged in size from the tiny Microraptor, which was only around 80 centimetres (cm) long, to the mighty Argentinosaurus. Argentinosaurus weighed the same as over 12 African elephants and was up to 40 metres (m) long. Here are some more record-breaking dinosaurs.

THERIZINOSAURUS HAD THE LONGEST CLAWS. EACH ONE MAY HAVE BEEN AROUND ONE METRE LONG.

Dinosaur species are named by the person who first discovers and describes them.

SAUROPOSEIDON WAS THE TALLEST DINOSAUR AT AROUND 18 M.

FINDING THE EVIDENCE

Dinosaurs died out around 66 million years ago (mya). **Palaeontologists** rely on **fossils** for information about the dinosaurs.

HOW DO FOSSILS FORM?

Fossils form when dead animals are covered by mud or sand, soon after their death. Over millions of years, more layers of **sediment** build up. As sediment is buried under more layers, it is squeezed together until it turns into rock.

COMPLETE SKELETON FOSSILS ARE VERY RARE.

FOSSILS ARE EASILY DAMAGED.

PERFECT COPIES

Water, trickling through the rocks, wears down the bones. **Minerals** in the water then slowly replace the bones, leaving perfect rock copies of them. The rock layers covering the fossils are then worn away, allowing the fossils to be dug up.

Fossils have been found on every continent, including Antarctica.

Palaeontologists can use fossils to work out how large a dinosaur was, how it moved and even how it died. They can even tell the size and position of the muscles.

FOSSILISED POO

TRACE FOSSILS

Sometimes, all that's left is footprints or poo. These are called trace fossils. Fossilised dinosaur footprints give information about the size and speed of the dinosaur, whether it was moving in a herd or alone, and whether it walked on two or four legs. Fossilised poo can tell us what a dinosaur ate for its last meal.

THE MESOZOIC ERA

Dinosaurs first appeared near the beginning of the Mesozoic Era. The era began 252 mya and ended around 66 mya with a **mass extinction**. It was split into three periods: Triassic, Jurassic and Cretaceous.

TRIASSIC PERIOD (252–201 MYA)

THE EARTH'S LAND WAS MADE UP OF ONE BIG supercontinent, CALLED PANGAEA.

PANGAEA

The Triassic Period was hot and dry, with a bare desert landscape. Plants only grew along coasts or riverbanks. The earliest dinosaurs were tiny compared to the towering giants of later periods.

JURASSIC PERIOD (201–145 MYA)

During the Jurassic Period, the **climate** changed, becoming wet and **humid**. Forests, ferns and other plants sprung up thanks to the heavy rainfall. In turn, these plants helped some of Earth's biggest-ever land animals to grow. Meat eaters appeared too, along with the earliest-known bird, called Archaeopteryx.

ARCHAEOPTERYX WAS THE FIRST DINOSAUR WITH FEATHERS EVER DISCOVERED.

VELOCIRAPTOR WAS FAST AND FIERCE, USING ITS RAZOR-SHARP TEETH AND CLAWS TO BRING DOWN ITS prey.

CRETACEOUS PERIOD (145–66 MYA)

The Cretaceous Period saw the rise of huge, meat-eating dinosaurs, such as Tyrannosaurus rex. Plant eaters developed body armour, horns and spikes to protect themselves from these meat-eating **predators**. Bees, grass and flowers appeared for the first time.

HERBIVORES AND CARNIVORES

PLANT EATERS

Creatures that only eat plants are called herbivores. Herbivorous dinosaurs had many **adaptations** that helped them eat plants. Some, such as Brachiosaurus, swallowed food without chewing it. It may have swallowed stones, called gastroliths, to help it grind food in its stomach.

THE LONG NECK OF BRACHIOSAURUS HELPED IT TO REACH LEAVES HIGH UP IN THE TREETOPS.

EDMONTOSAURUS

Others, such as Triceratops, used their sharp beaks and strong teeth to eat tough plants such as palm leaves. Duck-billed dinosaurs, such as Edmontosaurus, had more than 1,000 tightly packed teeth to help them chomp quickly through tough plants.

MEAT EATERS

Creatures that eat mostly meat are called carnivores. Carnivorous dinosaurs were well adapted to hunt and kill prey. They had good eyesight with forward-facing eyes to help them spot their next meal.

BARYONYX HAD LARGE, POWERFUL CLAWS, AS THIS FOSSIL SHOWS.

Long, narrow jaws helped Spinosaurus to catch fish.

Carnivores had strong legs that were ideal for chasing prey at speed, while their chunky tails helped them to keep their balance. Powerful jaws helped them to grab and crush their prey. They also had sharp claws and teeth for stabbing and ripping flesh.

THEROPODS

Scientists put dinosaurs with similar features into groups. Almost all theropods, for example, were meat-eating predators. They included some of the largest carnivores that ever lived on land. Their name means 'beast foot' and was given to them because of the sharp, hooked claws on their toes.

ALLOSAURUS

Theropods all ran on their strong hind legs and used the clawed fingers on their short arms to grab and tear prey. Many theropods were fast and agile, with large eyes. A few theropods, such as Caudipteryx, were omnivores, meaning that they ate both plants and animals.

Small theropods **evolved** over millions of years into modern-day birds.

CAUDIPTERYX

TYRANNOSAURUS REX

Tyrannosaurus rex, often called T. rex, was a theropod that lived in the Late Cretaceous Period. Using its 60 saw-edged, pointed teeth and powerful 1.2-metre-long jaw, it could eat up to 230 kilograms (kg) of meat in a single mouthful.

EACH TOOTH WAS ABOUT 20 CM LONG. THIS IS ABOUT THE LENGTH AS AN ADULT HUMAN'S HAND.

T. rex had a larger brain than most dinosaurs, helping it to be a clever, successful hunter at the top of the **food chain**.

THE DIAMETER OF EACH T. REX EYEBALL WAS AROUND EIGHT CENTIMETRES – THE SIZE OF AN ADULT HUMAN'S FIST.

T. rex's bite was around three times as powerful as that of a lion, and fossilised poo shows that it crunched its way straight through the bones of its prey. It used its excellent sense of smell to track down both live prey and dead animals to **scavenge**.

THYREOPHORANS

Thyreophorans were plant-eating dinosaurs that walked on four legs. They included two main groups – stegosaurs and ankylosaurs. Although they moved slowly, they were not easy targets for carnivores, thanks to the armoured plates and protective spikes on their bodies and tails.

Ankylosaurus had a heavy club on its tail which it used to whack predators.

Kentrosaurus had seven pairs of plates on its neck and back and a set of spikes on its back and tail. The tail was extremely bendy and could be swung round with force to fight off an attacker.

KENTROSAURUS HAD SPIKES ON ITS SHOULDERS TO PROTECT IT FROM ATTACKS FROM THE SIDE.

STEGOSAURUS

Stegosaurus was a thyreophoran that lived in the Jurassic Period. It had thin, bony plates, called scutes, in the skin along its back. These plates could have been used to attract a **mate**, scare off predators, or control body temperature.

Stegosaurus was a huge dinosaur, reaching nine metres in length, but it had a tiny brain around the size and shape of a small, bent sausage. The spikes at the end of its tail pointed outwards for protection.

Stegosaurus needed to eat huge amounts of food, such as bushes and mosses, to keep its enormous body going.

SAUROPODS

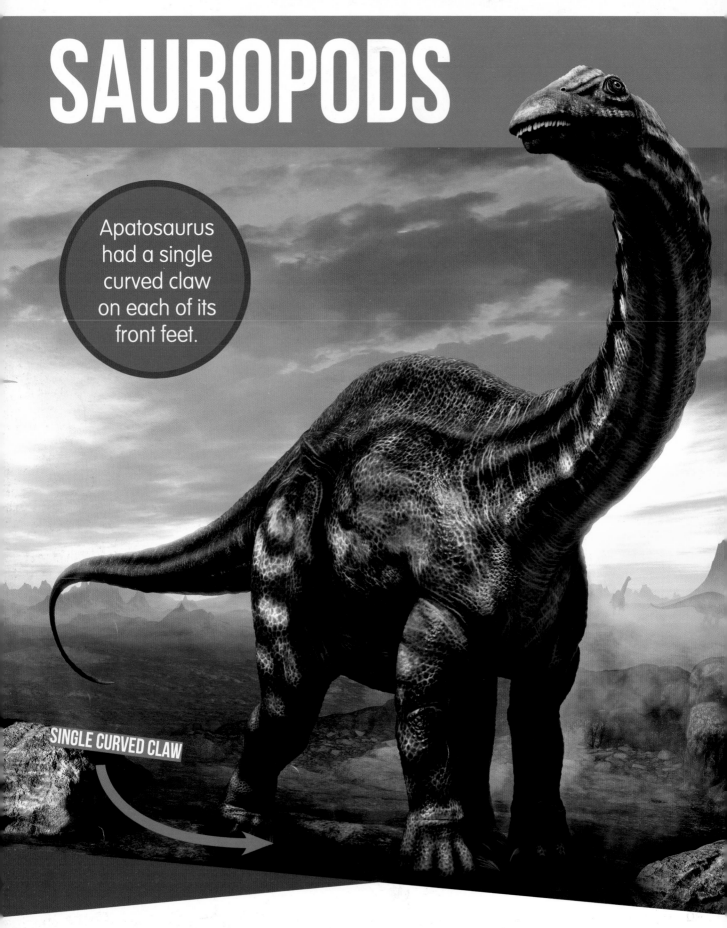

Apatosaurus had a single curved claw on each of its front feet.

SINGLE CURVED CLAW

Sauropods were the largest land animals that ever lived on Earth. They were herbivores with long tails and a small head on an extremely long neck. Light, mostly hollow neck bones, a giant body and a sturdy four-legged standing position helped them to support their huge necks. Their massive size meant that they needed to eat lots of food throughout the day. Fossilised footprints show that sauropods lived in herds for safety.

DIPLODOCUS

Diplodocus was a giant sauropod that lived in the Late Jurassic Period. It was around 26 m long from head to tail and weighed 20,000 kg. A bendy neck allowed it to reach food high up in the trees and low down on the ground.

Diplodocus could whip its tail to make a booming sound, which may have scared off attackers.

Diplodocus had rows of peg-like teeth that looked like a comb, which it used to strip leaves from plants. Despite its massive weight, it could rear up on to its back legs, supported by its tail, to reach the highest branches.

ORNITHOPODS

Ornithopods were plant eaters that lived during the Jurassic and Cretaceous Periods. Most ornithopods walked on two legs, but some may have walked on four. Many had beaks for collecting leaves. Their name means 'bird feet'. The earliest ornithopods were small and nimble, reaching only one metre in length. Later, they evolved into much larger creatures that were up to 15 m in length.

CORYTHOSAURUS

HOLLOW CREST

PARASAUROLOPHUS

Corythosaurus lived during the Cretaceous Period and grew up to 10 m long.

THE CREST OF PARASAUROLOPHUS COULD GROW TO 1.8 M LONG.

Parasaurolophus had a narrow, hollow crest on its head that made its deep calls echo, so that they sounded louder.

IGUANODON

Iguanodon was an ornithopod that lived in the Early Cretaceous Period. It had a horny beak for collecting leaves and strong back legs that helped it to walk either on four or two legs. Iguanodon had thumb spikes on its front feet, which may have been used for protection or gathering food.

It was given its name, which means 'iguana tooth', because its teeth looked like those of a modern-day lizard called an iguana, although iguanas are much smaller.

FOSSILISED IGUANODON TEETH

CERATOPSIANS

Ceratopsians were herbivores with enormous heads that lived in the Cretaceous Period. Many had bony frills and horns around their faces and parrot-like beaks for gathering food. Their name means 'horned face'.

Einiosaurus had two spiky horns sticking out of its frill and a long, curved horn on its nose.

THE SKULL OF PENTACERATOPS MEASURED OVER THREE METRES FROM THE TOP OF THE FRILL TO THE TIP OF THE NOSE.

The horns were used to fight off predators and scare off other attackers, while their frills made them look bigger and more attractive to a mate. Scientists think that horns and frills may also have helped them to recognise other members of their herd.

TRICERATOPS

Triceratops was a ceratopsian that lived in the Late Cretaceous Period. It had a large, protective frill that was up to one metre across, as well as three horns – one on its nose and two on its head.

The frill may have been brightly coloured.

FOSSILS SHOW THAT T. REX COULD BITE THROUGH THE HORNS OF TRICERATOPS.

Males may have used their horns to impress females and fight with other males. Triceratops consumed hundreds of kilograms of plant material every day. They could grow up to nine metres in length and to a weight of 5,500 kg. It may have used its bulky body to knock over small trees for food.

PACHYCEPHALOSAURS

Pachycephalosaurs were herbivores that lived in the Late Cretaceous Period. Their name means 'thick-headed lizard' and it was given to them because they had very thick skulls that were either flat or domed, like bowling balls.

Despite having such a thick skull, pachycephalosaurs had a tiny brain.

Pachycephalosaurs travelled on two legs, using their long tails for balance. They had small peg-like teeth and ate food that grew close to the ground, such as seeds, stems, leaves and fruits. Bony spikes on the snout and along the back of the skull gave some protection from predators.

COMPLETE FOSSILS OF PACHYCEPHALOSAURS ARE VERY RARE.

PACHYCEPHALOSAURUS

Pachycephalosaurus was the largest of the domed dinosaurs. It grew to around eight metres in length and weighed about 3,000 kg. Its domed skull was an amazing 25 cm thick. Experts have different ideas about what Pachycephalosaurus used its domed skull for. Some think it was used by males to show off to other males or to attract a mate. Others think it was used for head-butting rivals or as defence against predators. They may have even used it to recognise each other.

No dinosaur had a skull thicker than Pachycephalosaurus did. Its skull was around 20 times thicker than any other dinosaur's!

PACHYCEPHALOSAURUS MAY HAVE FOUGHT OTHER MEMBERS OF THE SAME SPECIES BY HEAD-BUTTING.

TEETH AND FEATHERS

Unlike humans, dinosaurs continually grew new teeth throughout their lives. By looking at fossilised teeth, palaeontologists can tell how a dinosaur gathered its food, what it ate and how it chewed, slashed or ground down its food.

FOSSILS OF CARNIVORE TEETH OFTEN SHOW SIGNS OF DAMAGE, CAUSED BY CHOMPING THROUGH BONES AND BODY ARMOUR.

Giant plant-eating dinosaurs had to eat constantly to survive, so their teeth wore down quickly. These dinosaurs, such as Diplodocus, replaced their teeth about once a month and had up to five replacements lined up behind each tooth. As one fell out, another took its place.

The discovery of the fossilised remains of a dinosaur called Sinosauropteryx in 1996 proved for the first time that feathered dinosaurs had existed. Fossilised feather colouring was also found, which showed that Sinosauropteryx had a striped tail and orangey-red feathers.

FOSSIL OF SINOSAUROPTERYX WITH FOSSILISED FEATHERS

The earliest feathered dinosaurs could not fly. They only used the feathers for warmth and for showing off. The first dinosaurs with wings that could flap, such as Archaeopteryx, appeared in the Jurassic Period, but they were weak fliers.

Microraptor probably used its feathered limbs to glide rather than fly.

EGGS, BABIES AND
PARENTS

All dinosaurs laid round or oval eggs with hard shells. The largest eggs, for example those of Apatosaurus, were about 30 cm tall, which is bigger than a basketball. Even these were very small compared to the size of the parents, showing that dinosaur young grew quickly.

Some fossilised eggs contain the remains of unborn baby dinosaurs. This image shows what a young dinosaur may have looked like.

Some dinosaurs laid their eggs in a hole dug in sand. Others made raised nests from mud. Fossils show that some dinosaurs, such as Citipati, sat on their eggs to keep them warm. Others covered the eggs with plants that gave off heat as they rotted.

CITIPATI

DINOSAURS OFTEN LAID 20 OR MORE EGGS AT A TIME.

Some dinosaurs abandoned their newly laid eggs or left newly hatched young to take care of themselves. Others took great care of their young, protecting them from predators and feeding them. **FOSSILS OF A DINOSAUR CALLED PSITTACOSAURUS SHOW THAT IT CARED FOR ITS YOUNG FOR SEVERAL MONTHS.**

This model shows what a Maiasaura nest with young hatchlings might have looked like.

Large groups of fossils of Maiasaura, meaning 'good mother lizard', show that these dinosaurs laid their eggs in huge breeding colonies, nesting close to one another for safety. Fossils of baby Maiasaura show that they were fed by their parents.

HABITATS

Dinosaurs lived in many different **habitats**, including woodlands, plains and deserts. Lush forests growing alongside rivers and marshes were home to herbivores such as Diplodocus and to the carnivores that hunted them, such as Allosaurus. Swampy forests provided plenty of food for huge herds of duck-billed herbivores, such as Edmontosaurus.

HORSETAILS

Swamps were also ideal habitats for fish-eating dinosaurs, such as Spinosaurus.

Wide, open plains, covered with ferns and other **prehistoric** plants, were home to herbivores such as Triceratops, and to predators such as raptors and T. rex. Rush-like plants called horsetails grew in wetlands (low-lying waterlogged plains) and were food for Iguanodon and Hypsilophodon.

Deserts are harsh habitats, with little food and water, but some dinosaurs managed to survive there. The most well-known desert from the Mesozoic Era is the Gobi Desert in Asia. It's believed that the area was likely a desert with very few small plants during this time. Fossils found there show that Protoceratops, Velociraptor and Oviraptor could all survive desert life.

One of the most famous fossils ever found was discovered in the Gobi Desert and shows Protoceratops and Velociraptor fighting. The dinosaurs died, buried in a sandstorm or by a sand dune that fell on them – the perfect conditions for fossils to form.

Protoceratops probably ate cycads (woody plants with hard, stiff leaves).

THE WORLD HAS CHANGED A LOT SINCE THE MESOZOIC ERA. AT THAT TIME, THE SAHARA, THE MODERN WORLD'S LARGEST DESERT, WAS A LUSH JUNGLE.

GOBI DESERT

29

DEATH OF THE DINOSAURS

Although they ruled the Earth for millions of years, dinosaurs were completely wiped out around 66 mya in a mass extinction. There are many ideas about how and why this happened, including gradual **climate change**. Scientists think the most likely explanation is that a giant **asteroid** crashed into the Earth.

The asteroid is thought to have been 10–15 kilometres wide and was likely travelling over 60,000 kilometres per hour when it smashed into Earth.

It may have caused volcanic eruptions, tsunamis, wildfires, earthquakes and dust clouds thick enough to block out the Sun's heat and light. Temperatures may have fallen and plunged the world into darkness, killing off plant life. Herbivorous dinosaurs would have then died out, followed by the carnivores that needed them for food.

A FEW CREATURES SURVIVED THE MASS EXTINCTION, INCLUDING SOME FISH, INSECTS AND THE ancestors OF MODERN BIRDS.

GLOSSARY

adaptations	changes to living things that happen over time and help them to be better suited to their environment
ancestors	animals in the past from which a modern animal developed
asteroid	a body of rock in space that normally orbits the Sun
climate	the common weather in a certain place
climate change	a long-term change in the typical weather or temperature of a large area
evolved	gradually developed and adapted to an environment over a long time
food chain	a series of living things that all rely on the last living thing as a source of food
fossils	parts of plants and animals that have been preserved in rock
habitats	the natural homes in which animals, plants and other living things live
humid	a warm, damp feeling in the air
mass extinction	a situation that results in a large number of living things dying out completely
mate	a partner (of the same species) that an animal chooses to produce young with
minerals	natural substances found in the Earth's crust
palaeontologists	scientists who deal with the fossils of animals and plants that lived very long ago
predators	animals that hunt other animals for food
prehistoric	something from before written history
prey	animals that are hunted by other animals for food
reptiles	cold-blooded, scaly animals that have a backbone
scavenge	to feed on other animals that are already dead
sediment	small pieces of a solid material, for example sand, that can form a layer of rock over time
species	a group of very similar animals or plants that are capable of producing young together
supercontinent	a mass of land that broke apart to create the continents that exist today

INDEX